LENGTH WORD PROBLEMS

Helen Mason

Crabtree Publishing Company

www.crabtreebooks.com

Writing team: Helen Mason, Reagan Miller, Crystal Sikkens
Publishing plan research and development:
    Sean Charlebois, Reagan Miller
    Crabtree Publishing Company
Editors: Ruth Frederick, Leslie Jenkins, Phyllis Jelinek
Proofreaders: Lisa Slone, Kelly McNiven
Editorial director: Kathy Middleton
Production coordinator: Shivi Sharma
Creative director: Amir Abbasi
Cover design: Margaret Amy Salter
Photo research: Nivisha Sinha, Crystal Sikkens
Production coordinator and prepress technician: Samara Parent
Print coordinators: Katherine Berti, Margaret Amy Salter

Photographs:
Cover: Thinkstock; Page 1: Levent Konuk / Shutterstock; Page 4: Yuri
Arcurs / Shutterstock.com; Page 5: Ziga Lisjak / iStockphoto.com (t);
Page 6: Yuri Arcurs / Shutterstock.com; Page 11: Yuri Arcurs /
Shutterstock.com; Page 12: TRINACRIA PHOTO / Shutterstock.com (l);
Page 12: Igor Sokolov (breeze) / Shutterstock.com (r); Page 13: kali9 /
iStockphoto.com; Page 17: Dominik Hladik / Shutterstock.com; Page 19:
Andrey_Kuzmin / Shutterstock.com (t); Page 19: michaeljung /
Shutterstock.com (b); Page 20: DNY59 / iStockphoto.com; Page 21: Denis
Vrublevski / Shutterstock.com (t); Page 21: Eric Isselee / Shutterstock.com
(ct); Page 21: schankz / Shutterstock.com (cb); Page 21: Joy Brown /
Shutterstock.com (b).

Artwork Created by Planman technologies: Pages 5; 7; 10; 15; 16.

(t = top, b = bottom, l = left, c= center, r = right, ct= center top,
cb= center bottom)

Library and Archives Canada Cataloguing in Publication

Mason, Helen, 1950-
    Length word problems / Helen Mason.

(My path to math)
Includes index.
Issued in print and electronic formats.
ISBN 978-0-7787-1079-0 (bound).--ISBN 978-0-7787-1095-0 (pbk.).--
ISBN 978-1-4271-9198-4 (html).--ISBN 978-1-4271-9274-5 (pdf)

    1. Length measurement--Juvenile literature. 2. Word problems
(Mathematics)--Juvenile literature. I. Title. II. Series: My path to math

QC102.M37 2013   j530.8   C2013-902666-5
                                        C2013-902667-3

Library of Congress Cataloging-in-Publication Data

CIP available at Library of Congress

Crabtree Publishing Company

Printed in the USA/052013/JA20130412

www.crabtreebooks.com   1-800-387-7650

Published in Canada
Crabtree Publishing
616 Welland Ave.
St. Catharines, ON
L2M 5V6

Published in the United States
Crabtree Publishing
PMB 59051
350 Fifth Avenue, 59th Floor
New York, New York 10118

Published in the United Kingdom
Crabtree Publishing
Maritime House
Basin Road North, Hove
BN41 1WR

Published in Australia
Crabtree Publishing
3 Charles Street
Coburg North
VIC, 3058

Contents

Measuring Length and Height **4**

Units for Measuring **6**

Steps for Solving Word Problems . . . **8**

Solving Measurement Problems . . . **10**

Solving More Than One Way **12**

Solving with a Number Line **14**

Measuring a Birthday Banner **16**

The Jumping Game **18**

More Word Problems **20**

Glossary **22**

Index and Learning More **24**

Measuring Length and Height

Today is Lynn's birthday. She is eight years old.

On her birthday each year, Lynn's father, Mr. Carter, measures her **height** to see how much she has grown. Height is how tall or high something is.

There are different tools that can be used to measure height or **length**. Length is how long something is.

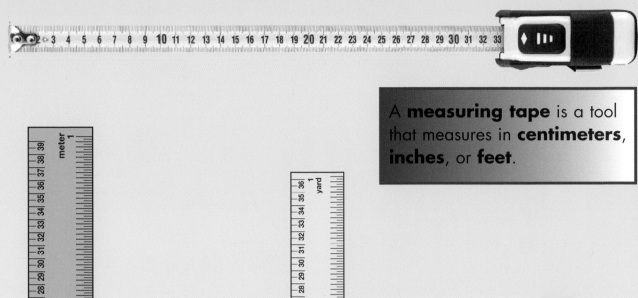

A **measuring tape** is a tool that measures in **centimeters**, **inches**, or **feet**.

A meterstick is a tool that measures in centimeters and **meters**.

A yardstick is a tool that measures in inches, feet, and **yards**.

A **ruler** is a tool that measures in centimeters and inches.

Units for Measuring

Mr. Carter uses a measuring tape to measure Lynn's height. He measures from the floor to the top of Lynn's head. Lynn is 50 inches, or 127 centimeters, tall.

Lynn wonders why her height is more in centimeters than in inches. Her dad tells her that you can measure height in different **units**, such as centimeters, inches, feet, and meters. The size of each unit is not the same. He makes a chart to help Lynn understand.

	A centimeter is about the width of your finger.
	An inch is about the width of two of your fingers.
	A foot is about the height of this book.
	A meter is about the height from the floor to a door knob.

Lynn sees that one finger equals about one centimeter and two fingers equal about one inch. This means that a centimeter is shorter than an inch. So it takes more centimeters to measure her height than inches.

Activity Box

Lynn measures the length of one of her birthday gifts. It is 11 inches long. Would the gift be bigger or smaller if it was 11 centimeters? Would the gift be bigger or smaller if it was 11 feet?

Steps for Solving Word Problems

Lynn's friend Huan asks her to solve his birthday riddle. Lynn is not sure where to begin. Huan teaches her four steps he learned in school for solving word problems.

Huan's Birthday Riddle

Riddle me. Riddle me.
See if you know.
Last year you were 45 inches.
How much did you grow?

Steps to Solving Word Problems

1. **UNDERSTAND** – What does the problem ask you to do? What information do you have to solve it?

2. **PLAN** – How can you solve the problem? What **operations** will you use? Set up the problem using numbers, pictures, or a model.

3. **SOLVE** – Do the math.

4. **CHECK** – Does the answer make sense?

Huan explains that the first step to solving a word problem is to understand what the problem is asking and find the information you need to solve it.

Lynn reads the riddle again. She draws a circle around the measurement and highlights the question. Huan tells her there is a piece of information that is missing.

What else does Lynn need to know in order to solve the problem?

Riddle me. Riddle me.
See if you know.
Last year you were (45 inches)
How much did you grow?

Lynn's Thinking

I will need to know how tall I am this year to find out how much I have grown since last year.

Solving Word Problems	
✓	1. **Understand**
	2. **Plan**
	3. **Solve**
	4. **Check**

Solving Measurement Problems

Lynn decides to use blocks to build a **model** to help her solve the problem. Each block is 1 inch high. Lynn builds a tower that is 45 inches tall. This is how tall she was last year.

Since Lynn has grown taller, she knows she needs to add blocks to the tower. She adds one block at a time until the tower is 50 inches tall. Lynn and the tower are now the same height.

45 inches →

Lynn's Thinking

Last year I was 45 inches tall. This year I am 50 inches. I need to find out how many inches I grew.

Solving Word Problems

✓	1. **Understand**
✓	2. **Plan**
	3. **Solve**
	4. **Check**

Lynn added 5 blocks to the tower. Lynn tells Huan she has solved his riddle. She writes it as a **number sentence**.

45 inches + 5 inches = 50 inches

Lynn has grown 5 inches since last year.

Does this make sense? Lynn checks. She knows she has grown taller not shorter. So, adding 5 inches makes sense.

Solving Word Problems

✓	1. **Understand**
✓	2. **Plan**
✓	3. **Solve**
✓	4. **Check**

Activity Box

Last year Huan was 56 inches tall. He is now 60 inches tall. How much has Huan grown? Look at the number sentences below. Which one is the answer? How do you know?

56 inches + 4 inches = 60 inches

56 inches − 4 inches = 52 inches

Solving More Than One Way

Lynn asked for a hockey stick for her birthday. Mr. Carter takes Lynn and Huan to the store to choose one. Lynn finds two sticks she likes. The blue stick is 46 inches long. The yellow stick is 53 inches long. Mr. Carter asks them how much longer is the yellow stick than the blue stick? Both Lynn and Huan think about how they would solve the problem.

Lynn's Thinking

I know the blue stick is 46 inches long. How many more inches would I need to add to make it the same length as the yellow stick?

Lynn tells her dad that her number sentence is:

46 inches + X = 53 inches

Huan's Thinking

I know the yellow stick is 53 inches and the blue stick is 46 inches. I can subtract the length of the shorter stick from the longer stick to find the difference.

Huan then shares his number sentence:

53 inches – 46 inches = X

Huan and Lynn ask Mr. Carter which number sentence is correct. He says they are both right, and they should get the same answer when they finish solving the problem.

Activity Box

There is often more than one way to solve a word problem. Which number sentence would you use to solve this problem?

Solving with a Number Line

After shopping, Lynn and Huan each make a plan to solve the word problem. Lynn draws a number line to help her find the answer.

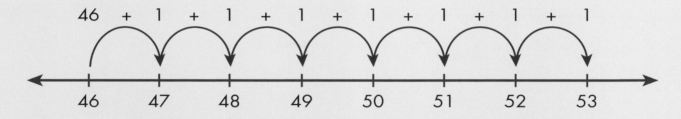

Lynn starts her number line at 46 inches, which is the length of the blue hockey stick. She counts forward by one until she reaches 53 inches. This is the length of the yellow hockey stick.

46 inches + X = 53 inches

What number is X in Lynn's number sentence?

Huan decides to use the inch blocks to help him solve his number sentence. He builds two rows of blocks. One row is 53 blocks long to show the length of the yellow hockey stick. The other row is 46 blocks long to show the length of the blue hockey stick.

To find the difference in length, Huan removes blocks from the longer row until it is even with the shorter row. He counts each block as he takes it away.

53 inches – 46 inches = X

What number is X in Huan's number sentence?

Did Lynn and Huan have the same answer?

Activity Box

Lynn's new hockey stick is 53 inches long. It is 9 inches longer than her old stick. Find two ways to solve this problem.

Measuring a Birthday Banner

Huan and his friend, Ella, want to decorate for Lynn's birthday party. They have a Happy Birthday banner to hang on the wall in the living room. Lynn's mom already has balloons and streamers hanging from two of the walls. Huan and Ella's banner is 6 feet long. They need to measure the two empty walls to see where the banner will fit.

Banner Word Problem

Wall A is 8 feet long, but there is a bookshelf that covers 3 feet of the wall. Wall B is 10 feet long, but there is a window that covers 2 feet of the wall. Which wall is the best place to hang the banner?

To find out how much space is left for their banner on Wall A, Ella subtracts the length of the bookshelf from the total length of Wall A.

8 feet – 3 feet = 5 feet

To find the space left on Wall B, Huan subtracts the length of the window from the total length of Wall B.

10 feet – 2 feet = 8 feet

On which wall were Huan and Ella able to hang the banner?

Activity Box

Lynn's mom gave Huan and Ella tools to measure the living room walls. She gave them a meter stick, a measuring tape, and a ruler. Which tool would you use to measure the wall? Explain your thinking.

The Jumping Game

The guests at Lynn's birthday party play a jumping game to see who can jump the farthest.

Lynn knows there are two parts to solving this problem.

Jumping Problem

Abby jumps 89 centimeters. Ella jumps 8 centimeters farther than Abby. Cameron jumps 13 centimeters less than Ella. How far did Cameron jump?

Lynn's Thinking

First I need to find out how far Ella jumped. I will use this answer to find the length of Cameron's jump.

Ella's jump:

89 centimeters + 8 centimeters = X

Lynn uses the tape measure to count forward 8 centimeters. Ella jumped 97 centimeters. Now that Lynn knows the distance of Ella's jump, she can find the length of Cameron's jump.

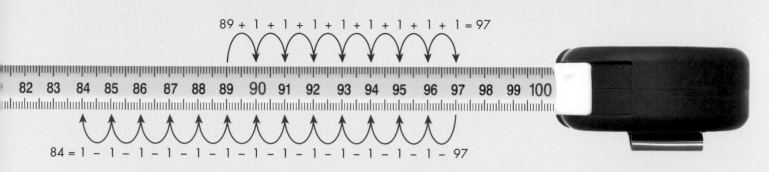

$$89 + 1 + 1 + 1 + 1 + 1 + 1 + 1 + 1 = 97$$

$$84 = 1 - 1 - 1 - 1 - 1 - 1 - 1 - 1 - 1 - 1 - 1 - 1 - 1 - 97$$

To find the length of Cameron's jump, Lynn starts at 97 centimeters and counts back 13 centimeters.

97 centimeters − 13 centimeters = X

How far did Cameron jump?

More Word Problems

Lynn received some books for her birthday. The books were about different plants and animals. See if you can answer these word problems on plants and animals from Lynn's books.

The Tree Problem

A large evergreen tree was 20 feet high. A lumberjack cut off 8 feet from the top of the tree. How tall is the tree now?

The Plant Problem

A plant is 6 centimeters tall in the spring. By summer, it is 38 centimeters tall. How much did it grow?

The Snake and Worm Problem

A snake is 86 inches long.
A worm is 5 inches long. What is the difference in length between the snake and the worm?

The Giraffe Problem

A mother giraffe is 14 feet tall. The father giraffe is 3 feet taller than the mother. Their baby is 11 feet shorter than the father. How tall is the baby giraffe?

Glossary

centimeter A unit of measure. There are 100 centimeters in a meter.

foot A unit of measure that is equal to 12 inches. One foot is about $\frac{1}{3}$ of a meter.

height How tall or high something is

inch A unit of measure. There are 12 inches in a foot and about $2\frac{1}{2}$ centimeters in one inch.

length How long or wide something is

measuring tape A tool used to measure

meter A unit of measure. One meter is about 3 feet 3 inches.

model Something that represents something else; usually as a smaller version

number sentence A sentence written using math and number symbols.

operation A mathematical process

ruler A tool that is used to measure. Most rulers measure up to 12 inches, or 1 foot. Some rulers also have centimeter markings.

units Lengths used to measure

yard A unit of measure. There are 3 feet (36 inches) in a yard. A yard equals about 90 centimeters or 0.9 meters.

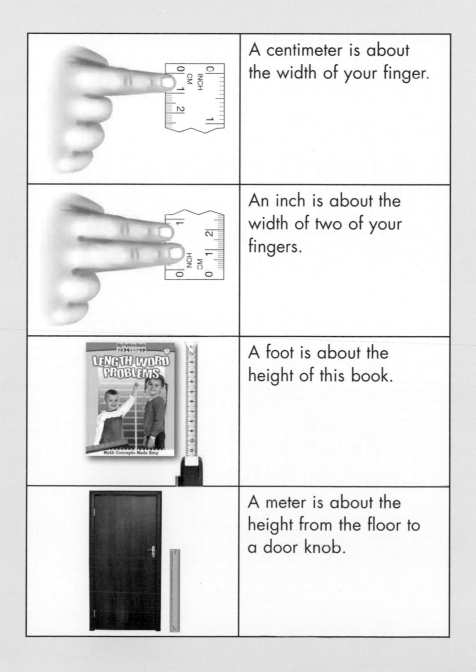

	A centimeter is about the width of your finger.
	An inch is about the width of two of your fingers.
	A foot is about the height of this book.
	A meter is about the height from the floor to a door knob.

Index

centimeters 5–7, 18, 19, 21

chart 6, 7

check 8–11

count 14, 15, 19

feet 5–7, 16, 17, 20, 21

height 4–7, 10

inches 5–7, 10–16, 21

length 4, 5, 12, 14, 15, 17

measuring tape 5, 6, 17, 19

measuring units 6–7

meters 5–7

model 8, 10

number line 14, 19

number sentence 11–15, 17, 19

plan 8–11, 14

riddle 8–9, 11

solve 8–15

understand 8–11

yards 5

Learning More

IXL

This site provides students with practice word length problems.

http://ca.ixl.com/math/grade-2/metric-units-of-length-word-problems

Math-Aids.com

This site provides worksheets to help students learn about units of measurement.

http://www.math-aids.com/Measurement/

http://www.math-aids.com/Measurement/Measuring_in_Centimeters.html

Beginner Word Problems

(My Path to Math) Minta Berry; Crabtree Publishing, 2012.

This book introduces the basics of solving word problems.

Measurement

(My Path to Math) Penny Dowdy; Crabtree Publishing, 2009.

This book introduces the basics of measurement.